DISCOVERING ME

ANDRE THOMAS

FOREWARD BY
DR. MORRIS CERULLO

Copyright © 2012 Andre Thomas

First Printing 2005, Second Printing June 2012

All rights reserved.

No portion of this book may be reproduced, stored in a retrieval system or transmitted in any form or by any means – electronic, mechanical, photocopy, recording, or other – except for brief quotations in printed reviews, without prior permission from the publisher.

www.greatnesspublishing.org

Published by Greatness Publishing, Ontario, Canada

Cover design by Farouk Roberts
Brands & Love Creative

Library and Archives Canada ISBN 978-0-9868878-6-4

All Scripture quotations are from the New King James Version of the Bible, except otherwise stated.

Foreword

I have ministered all over the world for over 50 years that God is a God of purpose, plan, design, and objectivity.

What a joy it is to see Bishop Andre Thomas guide his readers into this ultimate and essential discovery. What the world is seeking to accomplish through psychology, positive thinking and the worn-out idea of "building self- esteem," Andre exhorts believers to achieve through pressing in to know God's plan for our lives - a plan that does not depend on what we are in the natural, but what He can make of us.

Not from an ivory tower, but from a full week of prayer and fasting with the Lord, Andre brings forth in this volume his call to every Christian to 'Rise up and run your purpose race!'

I say Amen!!

Dr. Morris Cerullo

Table of Contents

Introduction

Chapter 1
Your Design   1

Chapter 2
Intrinsic Value – Add Pictures   4

Chapter 3
Your Inherent Value   6

Chapter 4
Understanding the Language of
Purpose   12

Chapter 5
Signposts of the World of Purpose   21

Chapter 6
Purpose and Service   27

Chapter 7
God Gives Purpose Descriptions   31

Chapter 8
Secrets To Discovering Your Purpose   41

Introduction

There is an epidemic of cataclysmic proportions in the world. It is an epidemic of poor self- esteem. Entire industries have been created to address this problem. Never in the history of the world have we had so many people saying in their own way, 'Make me feel good about myself', and using external things, without success, to make them feel good.

The problem is not a value problem; it is an ignorance problem, for many do not realize that you cannot make them feel good about themselves who already have poor self-perception. The key issue is to fix your self- perception problem. To do this there are certain facts about yourself that you must realize. Your self-perception must be based on the reality of who you are. In order for you to understand your value, you must understand your design.

Man is a creature and therefore has a Creator. He did not just appear. He is a creature of design. You were designed by a creator who is intelligent, has foreknowledge and who understood the challenges that your environment would bring to you. He pre-built in you the capacity to overcome the adverse effects of your environment. Man is the most sophisticated piece of machinery ever designed. To this day the full potential of this marvelous creature called man has not been realized (1John 5:4).

In this book you will receive the keys to understand and manifest your value and discover your purpose. Use them to unlock peace, wholeness, significance and fulfillment in your life.

Chapter 1
YOUR DESIGN

You Were Created!

In the beginning God created the Heavens and the Earth. Genesis 1:1

The word "God" in this text is Elohim or the Almighty Designer or Inventor. This text could translate: In the beginning, the Almighty Designer after He had designed the heaven and the earth, created them. You are part of His design. On the sixth day, He said "Let us make man in our image and our likeness" (Let us make man and design him to be like us).

Image and Likeness

Image in the context means, "Let us make man to have the same qualities that we have". Man was designed to have God's qualities. God has choice therefore man has choice; God is a speaking spirit therefore man is a speaking spirit; God is creative therefore man is creative.

God put His Attributes in Man

Likeness means a representative figure or a duplicate. God said, "Let man be a duplicate of us". There are some duplicates that are not made in the same image as the original. For example, I could make a duplicate Mercedes Benz, C class that is made of plastic. It looks like it, but it has none of the attributes the real Mercedes has. So when God said, let man have our likeness, it means, let what is in the original prototype be in the duplicate. God put into man what is in Himself.

Your value is found in your design. You are valuable because you are made in the image of divinity and your design is awesome. Whether or not someone hugs you or pays attention to you, by virtue of your design you are of infinite value. God also made man in His likeness so he could look on the outside like God does. Every individual looks like God.

"When the creatures moved, I heard the sound of their wings, like the roaring of rushing waters, like the voice of the Almighty, like the tumult of an army. When they stood still they lowered their wings. And then there came a voice above the expanse over their heads as they stood with lowered wings. Above the expanse over their heads was that like a throne of Sapphire, and high above on the throne was figure like that of a man." Ezekiel 1:24-26.

Who was in the appearance of a man? The Heavenly Father was, and, if you were made in His image and likeness, whatever He looks like, you look like. We look like God. God has the same anatomy we do.

What Color is God?

"And I saw as the colour of amber, as the appearance of fire round about within it, from the appearance of his loins even upward, and from the appearance of his loins even downward, I saw as it were the appearance of fire, and it had brightness round about." Ezekiel 1:27

**"And immediately I was in the spirit: and, behold, a throne was set in heaven, and *one* sat on the throne. And he that sat was to look upon like a jasper and a sardine stone: and *there was* a rainbow round about the throne,
in sight like unto an emerald." Revelation4:2-3.**

To the writer, the outer appearance of God looked like jasper, sardine stone, surrounded by emerald looking rainbow. God is definitely not one color. God shines. We are made in that likeness but not in the same glory.

Chapter 2
INTRINSIC VALUE

You are valuable because you have God's attributes on the inside of you and you look like God externally. When God was ready to redeem man, (the word redeems means to buy back) He paid a price that was equivalent to the value of man.

Adam and Eve, the Father and Mother of the Human race sinned against God and corrupted the image of God that was in him. This contaminated image then spread to their descendant's, mankind. Thus Jesus came to redeem and take back and purify the contaminated image of God. The image of God had been stained with sin and corruption. Jesus, in coming to the earth, shed His blood to redeem man. Only the Blood of God the Son was valuable enough to buy the human race back. He would not have sent Jesus if an angel could have done it. Therefore, your value exceeds that of an angel! Jesus shed His blood because only the blood could buy back those who had been made in the image and like of God.

You are so valuable. God put Jesus Christ on the cross to buy you back.

Why does God tell us to feed the poor, look after orphans

and visit the people in prison and clothe the naked? This is because when God looks at them, He sees Himself. Many people have lost their sense of value because of what they have gone through in life. Every person has intrinsic value that cannot be devalued. It can only be unrealized.

Your value is found in your uniqueness. Your fingerprint is different from any other person who has ever lived, and from every other person who will live. You are a creature with distinction.

Chapter 3
YOUR INHERENT VALUE & TRAGEDY

Tragedy does not have the power to alter your intrinsic value.

Your inherent value does not change because of tragedy. Take a $1.00 coin and leave it on the highway for one week and observe vehicles drive over that coin, snow falling on it, sewerage truck dumping sewerage on it. If at the end of one week, you take that coin to the bank, you would still receive $1.00 for it. The value of the coin did not change because of the battering of life.

Your inherent value does not change because of rejection, rape, molestation, abuse, bankruptcy, jail, or divorce. Your inherent value is God- given. No circumstances of life can beat it out of you. It is intricately woven into the very essence of your being. It is who you are. If you
are living and breathing, your inherent value has not changed.

We have examples in life. Jail did not erode the inherent value of Nelson Mandela; blindness did not erode the inherent value of Helen Keller. A nervous breakdown did not erode the inherent value of Abraham Lincoln.

You might have suffered a nervous breakdown, but just like Abraham Lincoln, you can bounce back and manifest your inherent value and be a blessing to people. There are countless others whose names have not appeared in history books who have not allowed tragedies and the fierceness of life's storms to destroy their perception of their value. The key to overcoming human tragedy is to understand that your circumstances and situations do not define who you are.

If you define yourself by your tragedy, you will end up a derelict, but if you define yourself by your destiny in God, you will rise with wings like an eagle.

There is a story in the Bible that illustrates this. It is the story of Amnon and Tamar was raped by her half-brother Amnon. From the moment of the rape she redefined herself according to the event. The scripture tells us in 2 Samuel 13: 19-20 that she put ashes on her head and tore her robe of many colors that was on her, and went away crying bitterly. And Absalom her brother said to her, "Do not take this thing to heart." But Tamar remained desolate in her brother Absalom's house.

This is a very sad story; Tamar allowed one situation to define her destiny and her life. Tamar was raped, which is terrible. However, her perception of the event brought about a greater tragedy.

Do not bury your identity in the graveyard of your

circumstance. You are not what happened to you, you are what God says you are, you have what God says you have and you can do what God says you can do.

Manifesting Your Value

You are responsible for manifesting your value. The responsibility for the release of your value is not found in the hands of another. Others may help you discover what you have, but until the full release of your value your life will not change.

There are four benefits of releasing your value:

1. God will reward you. Gal 6: 7-10.

2. Wise people will reward you. There are all types of relationships that will change overnight if the parties involved will begin manifesting their value to each other. (Marriages, friendships, employer- employee relations, etc.) "Seeth thou a man diligent in his ways he will stand before kings."

3. Your self-esteem will be positive.

4. Your self-respect will increase.

Your value is like a seed that must be cultivated to bring forth fruit.

He also said, "This is what the kingdom of God is like. A man scatters seed on the ground. Night and day, whether he sleeps or gets up, the seed sprouts and grows, thought he does not know how. All by itself the soil produces corn- first the stalk then the ear, then the full grain in the ear. As soon as the grain is ripe, he puts the sickle to it, because the harvest has come."

Again he said, "What shall we say the kingdom of God is like, or what parable shall we use to describe it? It is like a mustard seed, which is the smallest seed you plant in the ground. Yet when planted, it grows and becomes the largest of all garden plants, with such big branches that the birds of the air can perch in its shade." Mark 4: 26-32.

When cultivated, your value will produce fruit from which other people can feed. The light bulb is a fruit of the value of Thomas Edison; the car is the fruit of the value of Henry Ford; two thirds of the New Testament is the fruit of the value of Paul the Apostle; healed bodies are the fruit of the value of Benny Hinn.

Worldwide Christian television is the fruit of the value to Paul and Jan Crouch; the song "Shout to the Lord" is the fruit of the value of Darlene Zshech; leadership empowerment is the fruit of the value of John Maxwell; revival fires blazing around the world is the fruit of the value of Dr. Rodney Howard Browne and this book is part of the fruit of my value. It is time for you to manifest yours.

Your value is released in the problems you solve for others.

The selfish never fully manifest their value because they are consumed with receiving value from others and giving nothing in return. This attitude cripples marriages, churches, families, companies and nations. A mango cannot eat itself and neither can you.

No person is complete within himself and is by divine design dependent on the goodness of God and the divinely granted abilities in his fellowman. This is beautifully portrayed in the story of the creation of Eve in Genesis 2 to help Adam. She was created primarily to add value to him. You have a divine deposit in you that when it is released will solve problems for others.

Your eternal value is manifested when you arise and fulfill your God given purpose. In the following chapters we will discover how to do just that.

I charge you!

Arise and release your value to your generation for:

RELEASED VALUE MOVES YOU FROM:

- ✓ **Obscurity to significance**
- ✓ **Victim to victor**
- ✓ **Poverty to riches**
- ✓ **Disrespect to respect**
- ✓ **Irrelevance to relevance**
- ✓ **And Eternal reward!**

Chapter 4
UNDERSTANDING THE LANGUAGE OF PURPOSE

The word ***purpose*** suggests an intention, a specific end to be achieved. Purpose is at the root of everything God does. He creates each person for a specific purpose. Purpose is the reason for which you were created. You are a product of God. When God calls you, He invites you to fulfill your purpose; the reason for which He made you.

Your purpose is the root of your life. From it springs the branches of potential, vision, destiny, identity and value.

Potential suggests possibilities i.e. things you can do or achieve but have not yet done or achieved. It is what you can be, do and have if you keep on developing yourself. There is Godly potential and ungodly potential. We all have the potential to do good, or the potential to do evil. Godly potential is the capacity or ability to do things that God has ordained for us to do. Ungodly potential is the capacity to sin. Your purpose determines your innate (inborn) potential.

Vision in this context is defined as a clear mental portrait of a preferred future. It is possible to have a "heavenly vision" of an "earthly vision." Paul tells us in Acts 28:18 that he was not disobedient to the heavenly vision.

The heavenly vision is God's purpose for you revealed in pictures that you can articulate, write down and move towards.

The earthly vision may or may not be a good idea. It may be an evil idea. Paul's earthly vision was to kill Christians, but God's heavenly vision for him was to be the writer of two-thirds of the New Testament, to plant churches all over the Gentile world and to be an apostle and a teacher of the Gospel.

Your earthly vision and your heavenly vision will clash. You can join the ranks of men and women like Saul who, realizing God's picture of him, decided to live his life for the fulfillment of the divine purpose picture called "vision".

Destiny implies a predetermined end and a course of events leading to that predetermined end.

There is *divine destiny* which is the glorious end

God has established for you. There is also *human destiny*, which is the end that your environment allows you to experience. *Satanic destiny* is the end that Satan has planned for you.

Identity addresses the concept of how you describe your individuality, the descriptions or characteristics you use to distinguish yourself from others. Your identity is based either in a Godly origin, or in a human origin. Men and women of divine purpose base their identity on their purpose.

You are more than a black man

You are more than a blonde bombshell

You are more than a size 22

You are more than an engineer

You are more than the wife of Mr. Wonderful

You are more than an Arab

You are more than a victim.

You are a distinctly, unique individual made in the image of God. Celebrate and wear your purpose. It is your distinction from all the people that have ever lived and will ever live.

Value defines worth. There is inherent value, and there is manifested value. The inherent value of an item is determined by its relevance to something or someone else.

God did not create anything complete within itself. Everything God creates provides a solution for something or someone else. The same principle applies to people. Everyone is created valuable, and within each person are solutions for other individuals and for the human race. We are all precious and priceless, but not everyone manifests this.

I declare by the Spirit of God that your inherent value on the inside of you will become manifested value!

When you start manifesting your value, your life will change!

When you start manifesting your value, the parasites in your life will leave!

When you start manifesting your value your days of God-size living have only just begun!

When you choose to manifest your inherent God-given value, your dominant gifts arise to the surface!

When you choose to manifest your God-given value, you move from being tolerated to being celebrated!

QUESTIONS

Potential

In the space below, write out what you can be, do and have if you keep developing the gifts God has given you.

_____

_____

_____

_____

_____

_____

_____

_____

_____

_____

1. Describe your perceived vision for your life.

_____

_____

_____

_____

_____

2. Would you say this vision is:

    a. A God idea
    b. A good idea
    c. An evil idea
    d. Not sure

Destiny

What do you think is your divine destiny?

_____

_____

_____

_____

_____

Identity

What distinguishes you from everyone else in the human family?

_____

_____

_____

_____

_____

Value

a. How would you describe your inherent value or relevance?

_____

b. Are you manifesting it?

c. If you are, how are you doing it?

_____

_____

_____

d. If you are not manifesting it, what are you going to do to change that?

_____

_____

_____

_____

_____

Chapter 5
SIGNPOSTS OF THE WORLD OF PURPOSE

God pre-built in our spirits the potential to fulfill our purpose. There are many signposts in us that would lead us to the treasure of our purpose.

Innate Wisdom

Wisdom may be defined as "thinking thoughts, applying principles and taking steps to create what you desire". Everyone has innate wisdom in certain aspects of life. Artists have artistic wisdom, musicians have musical wisdom, good preachers have mass communication wisdom, film directors have creative wisdom, and good team counselors have intra-personal wisdom.

If you go to a nursery and watch the children play for a prolonged period of time, you will see those that have creative wisdom, those that have leadership wisdom, artistic wisdom and interpersonal wisdom. This innate wisdom is evidenced from birth and if parents know what to look for, the signposts of innate wisdom will point them in the direction of their children's purpose.

Innate passion

Passion is associated with strong feelings and emotions. Not every cause or project will unlock your passion. Some may invoke your interest or sympathy, but very few will set you on fire. Those which set you on fire represent your innate passion. Passion is a signpost of purpose. Passion is a fuel for your purpose. God pre-built in you the passion to perform your purpose, and when you start moving towards your purpose, passion will arise from your heart.

Innate love

Love has been defined as the strongest emotion and as passionate admiration. It is the greatest force in the universe. Love is not passive. It propels, uplifts, motivates and sacrifices willingly, with a smile. You will never excel at something you do not love, and God pre-built in your spirit a love for your purpose.

When you discover your purpose, you will fall in love with it. You will have a love affair with your future. Innate love is a signpost of your purpose. There are many causes that can involve your emotions, but very, very few will unlock your love.

Innate gifts

Innate gifts are at times described as natural endowments and faculties. James 1:17 tells us that "every good and perfect gift is from above." These gifts are not taught but are given by God and can be developed. Without them you are like a boat without a sail.

Innate gifts are the raw material of potential. Your potential is found in your innate gifts and in the use and development of them. For example a person with administrative potential would have administrative gifts. There are different types of innate gifts.

Interpersonal gifting - men and women who are gifted to interact with people regardless of their economic status, class or ethnicity.

Technical gifting - people who work very well with their hands.

Numerical gifting - people who are skilled in tasks involving figures.

Communication gifting - they have skills in communication of ideas.

Administrative gifting - Decision making, problem solving, planning, organizing and supervising.

Artistic gifting - these people are involved in the arts, putting things and ideas together creatively. For example they excel in flower arranging, painting, decorating etc.

Musical gifting - Musical rhythms, melodies, voice or instruments.

Physical gifting - Athletic or sports abilities.

Intra personal gifting - The ability to connect with people's innermost feeling.

This list is by no means exhaustive, but it gives an idea of the various gift clusters that can be found in God's human product.

QUESTIONS

Innate Wisdom

In what areas do you have innate wisdom? (If you need assistance speak to a friend who is intimately acquainted with you).

_____

_____

_____

_____

_____

Innate Love

What causes unlock your innate love?

_____

_____

_____

Innate Gifts

What are your innate gifts?

Chapter 6
PURPOSE AND SERVICE

The word **ministry** is one of the most misunderstood words in the church today. It is merely "service". Your ministry is defined as the way God has called you to serve. God has raised up men and women to serve Him in every field of human endeavor. Purpose can also be defined as the solution you were born to serve people.

God has ordained for you to serve people. Acts 13:36 says "for David after he had served his own generation by the will of God, fell asleep". We are all called to serve people in a specific way.

- David served people as a warrior, king and a psalmist.
- Moses served people by leading the children of Israel out of Egypt, by writing the first five books of the Bible, and being the law-giver.
- Esther served people in the political arena by being a queen and by being used by God to save the Jewish people from extinction.
- Joseph served people by preserving the nation of Israel and by managing the food-stock during a

worldwide famine. Joseph's area of service was also in the political arena.
- Paul served people by preaching the gospel, building new churches and also writing two-thirds of the New Testament.
- Jeremiah served people by being a prophet to the nations.
- Mary Magdalene, Joanna and Susannah served people by providing financial and material resources to the ministry of Jesus.

"And also some women who had been cured of evil spirits and diseases; Mary (called Magdalene), from whom seven demons had come out. Joanna the wife of Chuza, the manager of Herod's household; Susanna; and many others. These women were helping to support them out of their own means." Luke 8:2-3.

- Peter served people by being an apostle to the Jews, leading the early church and by writing 1 and 2 Peter.
- Stephen served people by being a deacon in the early church (Acts 6:5).
- Dr. Luke served people by writing the Gospel of Luke and the Book of Acts as well as being a helper to the ministry of Paul the Apostle.
- Joshua served people by leading the children of Israel to possess the Promised Land.
- Bezalel, son of Uri, served people by designing artistic works in gold and silver for the Lord's house (Exodus 31).

- Aaron served people by assisting Moses, his brother and by being High Priest of Israel.
- Caleb served people through his service to Joshua.
- Timothy served people by serving the Apostle Paul and by being the leader of the church at Ephesus.
- Nehemiah served people by using his political office to rebuild the walls of Jerusalem.

Your greatest joy will be found in your area of service to humanity.

QUESTIONS

In what ways has God called you to serve people?

_____

_____

_____

_____

_____

_____

_____

_____

_____

Chapter 7
GOD GIVES PURPOSE DESCRIPTIONS

God does not want you to identify yourself by your giftings. He wants you to identify yourself by your purpose. In fact, the reason for your giftings is to equip you to fulfill your purpose. You can compare five men who have administrative gifts, but each one has a different purpose.

One could have a purpose to use the administrative gift in the political arena, another in the medical arena, another in the local church arena, another in the childcare arena, and another in the legal arena.

God gives gifts as equipment, but in order to discover your purpose, you have to look beyond your gifts. The gifts are merely equipment to fulfill your purpose and serve as signposts to what your purpose is. God is a God of definition.

He never leaves the definition of the product to the product. He is always very clear as to the original intent of the product. Let us look at the lives of some men and women in the Bible to whom God gave their job description.

When God made man He provided a job description.

"God blessed them, and said to them, "be fruitful and increase in number; fill the earth and subdue it; rule over the fish of the sea and the birds of the air, and over every living creature that moves on the ground." Genesis 1:28.

To be fruitful means more than to have children. It means every seed of potential inside you must bear fruit.

God is saying,

"I want you to see your fruit!"

"I want you to bear fruit with the administrative potential that I put on the inside of you!"

"I want you to bear fruit with the business potential that I put on the inside of you!"

"I want you to bear fruit with the artistic potential that I put on the inside of you!"

God is looking for fruit. He is looking for the product of your life.

"The Lord God formed man from the dust of the ground, and breathed into his nostrils the breath of life; and the man became a living being. Now the Lord God had

planted a garden in the east, in Eden; and the Lord God made all kinds of trees grow out of the ground--trees that were pleasing to the eye and good for food. In the middle of the garden were the tree of life and the tree of the knowledge of good and evil....The Lord God took the man in the garden of Eden to work it and take care of it." Genesis 2:7-9, 15.

The Lord God made man and then put him in the garden He had planted. It is amazing that God planted the garden and left it in an immature form.

In verse 15, God gave man his job description to tend the garden and keep it.God loves work. Work is holy, work is precious. Our Heavenly Father works!

"Thus the heavens and the earth were completed in their entire vast array. By the seventh day God had finished the work he had been doing; so on the seventh day he rested from all the work. And God blessed the seventh day and made it holy, because on it he rested from all the work of creating that he had done." Genesis 2: 1-3

The Bible tells us that God works. God worked for six days to create the earth then rested for one day. Many people want to rest for six days then work for one day! That is not God's pattern. You are not entitled to rest until you have produced. God, being a lover of work, the author and creator of work, put man in the garden to keep it and cultivate it. That was man's job description.

We see another job description actually given in Genesis 12: 1-3.

"The Lord said to Abraham, "Leave your country, your people and your father's household and go to the land I will show you.

I will make you into a great nation and I will bless you; I will make your name great, and you will be a blessing. I will bless those who bless you, and whoever curses you I will curse; and all peoples of the earth will be blessed through you."

Here we see God saying to Abram, "Your job, your purpose job description is to be the father of a brand new nation on the earth."

God does not leave you to figure out your purpose job description. If you come to Him He will reveal it to you. He is more passionate and committed to the revelation of your purpose description to you than you are to receiving it! After all, it is His idea!

We see Moses receiving his purpose description in Exodus 3:5-10.

"Do not come any closer", God said. "Take off you sandals, for the place where you are standing is holy ground" Then He said, "I am the God of your father, the God of Abraham, the God of Isaac and the God of Jacob." At this, Moses hid his face, because he was afraid to look at God. The Lord said, "I have indeed seen the misery of my people in Egypt. I have heard them crying out because of their slave drivers, and I am concerned about their suffering.

So I have come down to rescue them from the hand of the Egyptians and to bring them up out of that land into a good and spacious land, flowing with milk and honey—the home of the Canaanites, Hittites, Amorites, Perizzites, Hivites and Jebusites. And now the cry of the Israelites has reached me, and I have seen the way the Egyptians are oppressing them."

God then sends Moses to take his people out of the land of bondage to the land of Canaan which was his job description. God not only gave Moses his purpose description, but explained his divine logic for sending him on this task of deliverance.

Joshua's purpose description is found in Joshua 1: 1-9.

"After the death of Moses the servant of the Lord, the Lord said to Joshua son of Nun, Moses' assistant: "Moses my servant is dead. Now then, you and all these people, get

ready to cross the Jordan River, into the land I am about to give to them—to the Israelites, I will give you every place where you set your foot, as I promised Moses. Your territory will extend from the desert to Lebanon, and from the great river, the Euphrates—all Hittite country—to the Great Sea on the west. No one will be able to stand up against you all the days of your life. As I was with Moses, so I will be with you; I will never leave you nor forsake you.

Be strong and courageous, because you will lead these people to inherit the land I swore to their forefathers to give them. Be strong and very courageous. Be careful to obey all the law my servant Moses gave you; that you may be successful wherever you go. Do not let this book of the Law depart from your mouth, meditate on it day and night, so that you may be careful to do everything written in it. Then you will be prosperous and successful."

Joshua's purpose description was to lead the children of Israel into their promised land and the Lord gave him guidelines on how to ensure that his purpose is fulfilled. Your purpose job description includes God's divine guidelines for you.

Samson's purpose description is found in Judges 13:3-5.

"The angel of the Lord appeared to her and said, 'You are sterile, and childless, but you are going to conceive and have a son. But you shall conceive, and bear a son. Now see to it that you drink no wine or fermented drink and

that you do not eat anything unclean, because you will conceive and give birth to a son. No razor may be used on his head, because the boy is to be a Nazarite, set apart to God from birth, and he will begin the deliverance of Israel from the hands of the Philistines."'

In this instance, his mother was informed of his purpose description before his birth. This still happens today.

In the New Testament, John the Baptist's purpose description was given to his father.

"But the angel said to him, 'Do not be afraid Zechariah; your prayer has been heard. Your wife Elizabeth will bear you a son, and you are to give him the name John. He will be a joy and delight to you, and many will rejoice because of his birth, for he will be great in the sight of the Lord. He is never to take wine or other fermented drink, and he will be filled with the Holy Spirit, even from birth. Many of the people of Israel will he bring to the Lord their God. And he will go before the Lord, in the spirit and power of Elijah, to turn the hearts of the fathers to the children, and the disobedient to the wisdom of the righteous to make ready a people prepared for the Lord."' Luke 1: 13-17.

I have had the privilege of meeting great men and women of God who are representing Him in various fields of human endeavor. Every man or women of heavenly distinction is an individual who understands their divine purpose description.

I have met some who know that their purpose description is to help someone to fulfill the commission God has given them. Some have purpose descriptions to work with children, to work in business arena, to work as inventors, in the ministry of helps, to administrate, to be a gospel singer, to work in the political arena or to raise finance to support the endeavors of one particular ministry.

Your purpose will not be clearly defined unless you receive your purpose description. God will communicate to you and describe what He wants you to do. Then every gifting you have will make sense, and you will then realize that he has built you innately for the fulfillment of this purpose description.

When I discovered my purpose description, all my giftings made sense. When I heard the words, *"Just as I called Moses to take a people from the land of bondage to the land of Canaan, so have I called you to take a people from bondage to greatness,"* the purpose puzzle was solved for me.

QUESTIONS

What communication has God given to you about your purpose?

_____

_____

_____

_____

_____

_____

_____

_____

_____

(Remember, your purpose is always to serve humanity. Purpose is the love of God in Manifestation through you in a unique way. God's purpose for you will always be linked to service of a person or people in general. No one has purpose

that is just for themselves. God saved you because He loves you, but God calls you because He loves someone else).

Chapter 8
SECRETS TO DISCOVERING YOUR PURPOSE

"Meanwhile, Saul was still breathing out murderous threats against the Lord's disciples. He went to the high priest and asked him for letters to the synagogues in Damascus, so that if he found any there who belonged to the Way, whether men or women, he might take them as prisoners to Jerusalem. As he neared Damascus on his journey, suddenly a light from heaven flashed around him." Acts 9:1-3

Before believers were called Christians they were known as followers of "The Way", because they preached the way to heaven, the way to prosperity, the way to joy and peace, the way to distinction, the way to a great marriage, the way to the truth of life.

Life was made for movement, and if there is no movement in your life you die. All men, and women, boys and girls are moving towards a goal.

Here was Saul on a journey through life, pursuing his own

earthly vision and goal, the annihilation of believers, and suddenly, a light from Heaven shone. The discovery of your purpose begins when light from heaven shines upon you.

"The entrance of your words gives light and gives understanding to the simple." Psalm 119:130.

The light of God's Word entering your heart today, the revelations and secrets of this book are exploding in your life and dispelling the darkness of ignorance in your mind.

"The he fell to the ground and heard a voice saying to him, 'Saul, Saul, why are you persecuting me?' And he said, "Who are you, Lord?" And He said, "I am Jesus, whom you are persecuting. It is hard for you to kick against the goads."' Acts 9:4-5.

Here we see Saul receiving an encounter with Jesus, where Jesus reveals Himself to Saul and asks him, "Why are you kicking against the goads?" (Another translation says "Why are you kicking against divine impulse)?"

This is Saul's first encounter, which was his new birth encounter, when he gave his life to Jesus. Saul was a man of action and understood that Jesus does not save us for inaction, but that salvation is a passport to purpose. Saul then asks Jesus a second question, and this sets him up for the vision encounter.

"So he, trembling and astonished, said, "Lord, what do you want me to do?" Then the Lord said, "Arise, go to the city, and you will be told what you must do." Acts 9:6.

Here is a secret. Your purpose will never be clearly defined to you unless Jesus is not only your Saviour to you, but He is your Lord. "Lord" implies ownership. You must come to a point where you totally give yourself over to Jesus, to hear you purpose for your life from Him. If you do not make Him your Lord, your interpretation of His purpose will most likely be flawed.

Only when a man or woman surrenders to the Lordship of Jesus and comes before Him, with no preconceived ideas, with no intent to negotiate with Him, but simply to hear the purpose for which they were made, with an open mind will the purpose of God be accurately understood, and the purpose description accurately received.

This is the problem many saints have. Many have come to me saying, "I have been praying to God, but I'm not really sure what my purpose is." No, God is not withholding your purpose from you. The Bible says,

"Ask and it will be given to you, seek and you shall find, knock and it will be opened to you." Luke 11:9.

God wants you to know your purpose, because you will have to stand before Him and give a purpose lifestyle account to

Him.

Your problem is that you are seeking God for His purpose, but His purpose is on the "Jesus is Lord" frequency, while you are on the "Me, Myself and I" frequency. There is no way I can connect to an FM station, when my radio is on the AM band.

Many people are attempting to receive their purpose descriptions from God when they are on the wrong frequency. They come with themselves on their minds when they should come with Jesus on their mind knowing that God's purpose is not about them, it is all about Him and the people He has called them to serve.

You will not clearly understand your purpose description unless you change from the "Me, Myself and I" frequency and surrender yourself before God and make yourself a living sacrifice, holy, acceptable to God, which is your reasonable service. Romans 12:1.

Come before Him and say, "Lord, I make You the Lord of my life. Anything You want me to start, I will start. I come before You with no preconceived ideas and notions. I lay down my life, my agenda, my dreams, and my ambitions before you. Reveal to me your purpose for my life; how you have ordained that I express your love to your people. Reveal to me how I am supposed to serve people. Reveal to me your original intent, and I will rise up and do it, in Jesus' name. Amen!

This prayer, when you pray it from your heart, will result in only one thing - the revelation of divine purpose. However, there are people who because of the business of their lives have such busy minds that they are unable to detect the voice of God to them. You might need to take some time aside, fast and pray. You might need to go to a hotel room, leave the children for a day or two and spend time before God until your mind gets quiet and your purpose is revealed to you.

When I got hungry to discover my purpose, I took a week off work, asked my wife and children to visit my sister-in-law and I remained at home alone for a period of five days. I fasted and prayed and spoke to no human being until my mind quieted down and I was able to detect the clear voice of God, revealing my purpose to me.

In retrospect, I could have detected my purpose years before, but my problem was that my mind was too noisy. One of the enemies to the discovery of your purpose is a busy mind. Your mind must quiet down in order to detect your purpose.

There is nothing more important in life after making Jesus the Lord and Savior of your life, than the discovery of your purpose, and after that, the running of your purpose race.

Surrender your life before God right now. Say "Lord, not my will, but your will be done." Understanding will flood your heart.

God's purpose for you is the best version of you.

Understanding that God's purpose for your life is your place of greatest fulfillment, productivity and impact in the realms of eternity. Your purpose is not a minus, but your purpose is the reason for which you were born.

I see fear banished from your life. I see you flinging yourself into the arms of the Lord. Let hunger rise in you. Let desperation for the discovery of your purpose rise on the inside of you. Cry out to God saying, "Show me my purpose, or I die!"

Let this desire drive you into the presence of the Most High. Let the very light of Heaven shine upon you so that your purpose will be made manifest.

When it is revealed it will look like God and also look like you. It will look like God because it will take your personal partnership with the Almighty God for it to be fulfilled. It will look like you because you were designed for it.

Then write down your purpose. Rise up and run your purpose race.

Your days of mediocrity are over. Your days of mere existence are over. Your days of living by default are over. This day you will arise and put aside your ambitions and let the plan and will of Heaven interlock with your hunger and obedience.

Become the vessel God has created you to be. Represent God with excellence in the field of human endeavor to which He has called you. Be a light, a person of distinction. Do exploits. Run the race that is set before you laying aside every weight and every sin that does easily beset you. Fight the good fight of faith and cross the line of completed divine destiny.

You will have a new beginning. Your life will be lived by design instead of by default. Your design was determined by God and is waiting to be discovered by you.

God sent Jesus Christ to give you an opportunity to begin again. Seize this divine opportunity and arise to the best version of you.

You were designed…

- For righteousness and not sin.
- For health and not sickness.
- For peace and not sorrow.
- For eternal significance and not eternal damnation.
- For wholeness and not secret pain.
- For wealth and not poverty.
- For divine destiny and not misfortune.
- For fulfillment and not frustration.
- For heaven and not for hell.
- You will experience God design for you! If you do not know Jesus Christ as Savior and Lord, say this as a heartfelt prayer.

Dear Lord Jesus Christ,

I make you the Lord and Savior of my life. I believe you were raised from the dead for the resurrection of my divine destiny. I choose the destiny you have for me. Cleanse me from my sin and fill me with your Spirit.
Amen.

OTHER BOOKS BY ANDRE THOMAS

The 12 Spheres of Leadership (The 12 Types of

Leaders that Shape the Destinies of Nations) The Gift of Political Leadership
The Gift of Organizational Leadership

Unlock your Greatness
(A Young Leaders Handbook)

Uncommon Men and Distinguished Women
(A Rites of Passage Manual)

ABOUT THE 12 LEADER MOVEMENT

Purpose

To raise up a global movement of The 12 Types of Leaders that Shape the Destinies of Nations

Vision

To see a movement of The 12 Types of Leaders serve Heavenly solutions that shape the destinies of nations.

Mission

To raise up a global movement of The 12 types of leaders that shape the destinies of nations through events, partnerships, networking resources and online training.

How can my church, town, city or nation be transformed by 'The 12 Leaders Movement'?

There are 3 different events that Andre Thomas may be booked for:

1. Ideas and Solutions Church Conference.

This is our most comprehensive conference running for 3-4 days. Andre Thomas ministers in detail on The 12 Spheres of Leadership and also hold miracle, anointing and prayer services to see people delivered and activated into their leadership callings.

2. Leadership Sphere Seminar

This seminar runs for 1-3 days, depending on the needs of the host. Andre Thomas will focus on one particular sphere of leadership, chosen by the host. This seminar can cater to faith-based audiences or secular audiences.

*Customized workbooks will be available for purchase.

3. Speaking Engagements

Andre Thomas is also available for events that deal with any of the topics covered in the 12 Leaders curriculum.

www.anointingandwisdom.org

www.ingramcontent.com/pod-product-compliance
Lightning Source LLC
Chambersburg PA
CBHW072024060426
42449CB00034B/2250